# Torn Sky

# Torn Sky

*poems*

*Debra Nystrom*

Sarabande Books

LOUISVILLE, KENTUCKY

Library of Congress Cataloging-in-Publication Data

Nystrom, Debra.
    Torn sky : poems / by Debra Nystrom.— 1st ed.
        p.      cm.
    ISBN 1-889330-89-2 (hardcover : alk. paper) — ISBN 1-889330-90-6
(pbk. : alk. paper)
    1. West (U.S.)—Poetry. I. Title.
PS3564.Y78T67 2003
813'.54—dc21                                                                2002155511

Cover image: *East of Las Vegas, New Mexico, 1971* by David Plowden. © David Plowden, 1975. All rights reserved by photographer.

Cover and text design by Charles Casey Martin

Manufactured in the United States of America.
This book is printed on acid-free paper.

Sarabande Books is a nonprofit literary organization.

FIRST EDITION

For Dan and Mia,
and for my mother, my father, and Brad

# Contents

## I. The Cliff Swallows

## II. Secrets

# Acknowledgments

Grateful acknowledgment is made to the editors of the following journals and anthologies where some of these poems, sometimes in different form, first appeared:

*Anthropology and Humanism:* "Medevac: East From Eagle Butte," "Wounded Knee Creek: Hakiktawin's Story"

*The Bellingham Review:* "Regardless of the Final Score"

*Crazyhorse:* "The Tuesday Healing Service, Saint Mark's Mission Church"

*The Greensboro Review:* "Secretissime, Praesentissime"

*Heart:* "Keith's Dream"

*Meridian:* "To the Wizard"

*Michigan Quarterly Review:* "Half Time, Oglala High, 1970"

*Ploughshares:* "Waitress at a Window"

*Quarterly West:* "Thieves"

*Seneca Review:* "In Its Place," "Mother Listening"

*Shenandoah:* "The Cliff Swallows," "Fly-Fishing on Tommy's Lake," "Night Before the Fertility Clinic"

*The Southwest Review:* "Frieda's Plan"

*The Virginia Quarterly Review:* "The Girl Without Hands," "Leukemia"

*The Yale Review:* "Listening in Bed to You Reading *Swann's Way* Aloud"

"Regardless of the Final Score" also appeared in *Like Thunder: Poets Respond to Violence in America*, edited by Virgil Suarez and Ryan van Cleave, University of Iowa Press, 2002.

"The Cliff Swallows" also appeared in *Common Wealth*, edited by R.T. Smith and Sarah Kennedy, University of Virginia Press, 2003.

"Fly-Fishing on Tommy's Lake" also appeared in *Strongly Spent: 50 Years of Shenandoah,* edited by R.T. Smith, *Shenandoah*, 2003.

"Listening in Bed to You Reading *Swann's Way* Aloud," "Thieves," and "The Girl Without Hands" also appeared on *Poetry Daily*.

I would like to thank the Corporation of Yaddo, The Virginia Commission for the Arts, and The University of Virginia for time and space to work on these poems.

For specific help with all or parts of the manuscript I am most grateful to Renate Wood, Lisa Russ Spaar, Charles Wright, Greg and Trisha Orr, Deb Allbery, Laurie Kutchins, and especially Dan O'Neill, whose critical insights and suggestions were essential to the shaping of this book.

My sincere thanks to Tom Sleigh, Jennifer Ackerman, Karl Ackerman, Dinah Nieburg, Sheila McMillen, Michael Levenson, Gordon Braden, David Rivard, Alyson Hagy and Allen Peacock for their invaluable support and encouragement.

To everyone at Sarabande, to Jeffrey Skinner, and to my editor Sarah Gorham, for her faith in this book and her keen eye, very special thanks.

who makest the winds thy messengers,
fire and flame thy ministers
—Psalm 104

# Torn Sky

# I

## *The Cliff Swallows*

# Listening in Bed to You Reading *Swann's Way* Aloud

A dimmed coach-car carries me
along the curving rails

through violet-shadowed
swells of snow where

there are no signs,
no names; at the window

only the undulating white,
frame after frame unreeling

this question of time,
your voice speaking low

in sentences that throw
reflections, like those

at the drive-in movies
I was taken to in my pajamas,

and where I watched not the pictures
on the screen, but the shifting lights

as they passed over car hoods,
fanning through the dust-hung dark,

above the raspy noise
of the speaker-boxes

that could have been, say,
*The Bridge on the River Kwai*—

shouts, explosions, a flock
of mouths whistling,

all this something different
from what my parents in the front seat

heard and saw, and conjuring for me
exactly what I knew this dream to be:

the secrets of all brilliance
and sorrow flickering up

like swifts into the night sky.

# In Its Place

i.

my father hasn't met
the new neighbors yet
he's measuring to see if
the tree whose branch tore off
last night in the windstorm
is their poplar or his own
theirs he decides and gathers
what fell from his trees
dumps it in the pickup
but not that heavy sucker
it's theirs he leaves it
heads inside forgets his golf game
and the buddy waiting for him
he's going to watch out
the window wait and see what
kind of goddamned people will
leave their trash on his property
but he's not going
to be the one to speak

ii.

one of these days his brothers
and he have got to figure out how
on earth they're going to divide
their old man's land up

three decades Dad's managed
the business kept the home place
more than once from going belly-up
last week he drove out to Uncle Norm's
with Case parts and helped replace
the belt on the irrigation pump
they talked about crops and prices
till Dad started in about
getting a count of the chickens
certain some were missing
when he left
Norm got in his truck followed
him all the way back home
keeping just out of sight behind
sixty years since they had
any chickens on any farm


iii.


he reads now
he never read before
reads in his plaid TV chair
face set like he might be at
the tractor's wheel making passes
across an uncultivated field
page after page about the parts
of his life he once thought
just as well forgotten
about the Depression and Pearl
Harbor but also golf and Arnold Palmer
who was born the same year
he was came from nowhere

and nothing did everything with such
bass-ackwards will and never
was meant to amount to much


iv.


visiting Virginia visiting anywhere
makes him uneasy and now
it's snowing we're stuck inside
he keeps getting up from
our card game to look out the window
it's not so much restlessness though
as a kind of reluctant marveling
at the lack of wind
snow is a thing he knows
has shoveled frightened horses
out of tunneled through a whole day
from house to barn and blocked
from his face when after a week and
no sign he plowed through his Uncle
Albert's drifted-over road to find all
sixty cattle frozen in the windbreak
Albert in the tub wrapped in every
blanket he had alive but empty-eyed
he never spoke again
Dad lives in town now but even so
when it snows you don't see
the neighbors' place or anything
but a wild derangement of wind and ice
and air yet here on our deck
big fairy-tale flakes
falling straight down piling eight

inches straight up atop
the birdfeeder birds will find
the seed you can look out across
the even white to lights on in
the next house and the house
after that and everything seems
to be in its place

# Grandad

When supper was over he'd pull
the little pouch and bundle
of papers out of his pocket,
then peel free one white sheet
to fold into a tiny pair of wings across
his scarred left palm that twisted where once
the whole hand had torn off in a threshing machine.
With the right he'd loosen the drawstring,
and tap a narrow line along the crease. Roll the wings
together then, and pinch. Lick the seam.
Cracked lips puckered to the paper as he struck a flame
and puffed it into swirls hovering, then
fading above his head. Sometimes
he'd let me snug the string tight again.

# Homesteaders

After a while you'd stop talking
about the Old Country or the East—
like as not, the past went back

to somebody running from something,
needing to forget. This place
held no reminders, no blame.

Shadows of clouds stealing
across the plains, visible
from miles away, could be symbols

of nothing but the clouds themselves:
darkened only bunch grass,
buffalo grass, and tumbleweed,

then left them alone again.
Along the riverbed cottonwoods
flashing silver under-leaves in the wind—

what could they be signaling?
If you made it here you had
a hundred sixty vacant acres

to prove up, then claim for good; nobody
watching, only prairie larks
afloat like dust in the bottomless sky.

# *Toll*

*How many Indians from the Missouri tribes died of
smallpox . . . can hardly be estimated. Possibly one hundred
thousand.*

—Evan S. Connell
*Son of the Morning Star*

*No, Sven*—I couldn't part with it—
Mama had woven that blanket when she
sang me lullabies, and on the boat wrapped
herself inside its tulip-patterned blue
to ease the shivering and itching,
till the captain sent her bound in canvas
down through the waves. I hid it then.
*It's all I have left, Sven*—

      *—It's all, yes,* he hissed
*—we have to keep the food and tools,
and these people want what they haven't
seen before, they want pretty things,
and I won't be giving you to them.* Pretty
was a word I'd lost on the journey—
      *My face*—
Mama would sob into the blanket,
and I was glad we had no mirror on the passage.

Their chests glistened above the switch grass
outside the wagon; dark fists gripped
the ponies' manes, and I couldn't think
of those hands taking back to their tipis
what I had saved of her. For the first time
since I'd locked it, I lifted the pine trunk-lid
back on its hinges: *Live,* I heard
Mama whisper, *let them have it.*

# Regardless of the Final Score

No matter which side was more
battered and mud-smeared,
at Homecoming we cheered for game's end,
when the king and queen appeared
in eagle feathers and buckskin:
hundreds of palms drumming bleachers
as the royal pair lifted a torch-pole,
and flames snapped along gasoline-soaked
rags wrapping the goal posts.
We left them to burn, weaving
the snake dance down Main Street then—
a school of white kids flinging ourselves
along the dark, as if some current we couldn't
understand passed through us, like the impulse
of the showhorse Sitting Bull had accepted
from Buffalo Bill: when Lakota followers
crossed police about to arrest the old chief,
the rattled animal raised one hoof
as it had been taught, fluttered
its mane and spun to pace out
all the tricks it knew began with gunshot.

# Keith's Dream

*My father ran and fell down and the blood came out of his
mouth, and then a soldier put his gun up to my white pony's
nose and shot him, and then I ran and a policeman got me.*
—Herbert Zitcalazi
survivor, Wounded Knee, 1890

Keith's brother had a state-house job—
never told anyone they were Indian. Would've
killed Keith if he'd known the things
he told me, but no one was keeping track
of Keith much those last months.
After school, after wrestling practice,
after his shift at the D & E Diner
where he and the gory-aproned cook threw
knives past each others' ears in the wee hours
when the cook would start in again
calling him *Little Brain, Shitting Bull*—
around four he'd come to the window
to wake me, and we'd roll away across
the dark gravel, his muscles tensing
as he picked up speed out of town, headlights
tearing through grain dust, the two of us
imagining who we might be someplace else.
Once above the river he pulled off, leaned
his head against the gritty seat, asked if
I'd sleep awhile there in the car with him,
so he might not have the dream
of the boy playing on the pony when
the shooting began, or hear again the words
his grandfather used to say to him—
*They'll all come back one night—
the ghost shirts will bring them,
and the pieces of buffalo will bring*

*the buffalo, the land will be the way*
*it was again. We'll see that night*
*who the ghosts are. Don't let yourself*
*get any more white.*

We didn't sleep, we watched the light
creep along bluffs and buttes
puckering the tufted land above the river,
the place he said it would first
be renewed. We watched swallows lift
from below the bank. His hands were fists.

*In memoriam, K.E.O., 1954–1972*

# Four Sheets Cut Out

*We could see a great distance in every direction...high smooth
prairies and some fine bottom...gangs of buffalo at a considerable
distance.... We went the highest course to the River of Little
Children...proceeded on and struck our old track and returned
back to the pirogue about sunset...had a little rain this evening....*
—25 August 1804, journal of John Ordway
Sergeant Major, Lewis and Clark's
Corps of Discovery

*Four sheets...have been cut out...and only the stubs remain.*
—Gary E. Moulton, Editor
*The Journals of the Lewis & Clark Expedition:
Vol. 9, The Journals of John Ordway*

## 25 August 1804: After Floyd

Captain Lewis awake also. We set
the prairie on fire as a signal to the Sioux
to come to the river. Nothing yet
but silence, and now and then low flute-
like notes from the yellow-throated bird close by
every night since Sergeant Floyd's burial—
small meadow-skimmer of some kind; we haven't tried
to name it yet. No one speaks of Floyd; on the map we will
carry back his bluff is fixed; one of us will have to show
his people where we lit a flame on the mound
before shoveling, and took from his pocket the tow-
hair-bracelet that we found
to bring back to them. No more lashings in this dust,
I pray; the captains see how punishment divides us.

## 28 September 1804: Past Bad-Humored Island

High wind from southwest. Whitehouse has taken watch.
Myself dead-

exhausted, the pirogue still leaking a bit from its swing
    round with the current into
the barge. Bows strung along the banks, spears—Lakota, who
said we were bad medicine, seized our boat-cable, then
    begged us not to go ahead.
Today again the chief took the line, testing our nerve. Wind
    coming over in
gusts and rasps like throat-yowls of their dances, moccasins
    shifting the dirt,
pipe-smoke, tambourines rattling antelope-hoofs, the last
    tobacco-carrot
given by the captains not enough: drums thrown to the fire.
    Even
tonight on our boat anchored at the middle of the river
one chief sleeps with us. Captains remind him
he has promised to send his Omaha prisoners
back to their nation. No telling his intent.
Two elk swim
close by the boat in strong current.


## 4 October 1804: After Watch

As if flung down, men who have pulled all day
toward the unknown lie strewn beyond
sleep, floating their dreams over this land
of no hills, no trees, nothing but the laughing bay
of crooked-backed wolf-dogs, memory of bones—fish
skeleton longer than our keelboat knocking at
the cutbank. The river our own blood now, we pump
    against it
each day, against the heart we don't know yet except as wish,
as hope. Wind across these foreheads like a hand; lightning jolt
in the west; whiff of rain-pocks on dust the smell of Betsy's
mother's Bible—she opened it

*16*

to Corinthians, *we shall not all sleep, but we*
*shall all be changed*—shock of prairie-grass blown wet across
your face like unwept tears asking *do you feel this?*

## 31 August 1806: Vision, Return

Not one of us raised a hand or more than glanced
as we rowed past—Black Buffalo hooting after us,
lifting his rifle over his horse,
above the bank where the scalp-dance
shadows leered two years before.
Only the captain's insult shot across
the giddy current, as our parting this last
hostile place drove the oars
faster downriver than the river
itself could tumble toward the Omaha and home. Then
laughter; Frazier and Cruzatte began to sing; I shivered
and looked up: above us all a tearing open of sky, sudden
as the temple veil—sheets of arrowhead swallows shearing
   down,
then swerving past us to their riddled cliff. Then gone.

# Oahe Races

All the way out north
past the Indian turtle mound,
past the turnoff to the dam,
down the new-laid gravel stretch
through scrubby dry-land corn,
we watch the squall line shadow us
to the west, once or twice flicking
little lightning shocks—
a tease, keeping its distance.
It's summer, Sunday night
before more work. This is what
there is: not the rain that Dad
glumly begged for all week without
speaking it, without saying why
the cattle broke through Venner's
fence again over by the reservoir,
or asking why up by Agar
they got eighty-five hundredths
from the storms that blew through
Wednesday and we got
nothing—nothing but dust,
and you and me bumping through
dirt-track billows to
the grandstand that sways
over simmering asphalt rings,
its speakers rasping the "Star-Spangled
Banner" into grease-fumes and ear-
scorching motor-roar, continuous
unmuffled explosion of every
cylinder of every reined-in car—then

the shouts, and then the flag, the shot:
old double-barred rigs floored, geared
and blown-out, smoking furious circles
we follow without thought,
jumping up in gritty snake-boots,
haltertop, lipstick, sweat, heads rung,
throats seething a thrill not the same
as back-break and bull-throw of rodeo,
where we know our riders' grimaces,
hands tossed up by brother and cousins
to toast after—no, this spectacle's drivers
of blur and crush and blaze, lacquered
helmet thrown out from the heap,
are faceless from the bleachers, just
purse-seekers out of Mandan or Huron
or Aberdeen, offerings to flame,
or to the night's own heat,
or to the hollow growl behind it, spit
of moisture streaking our arms and cheeks,
then the windshield, headlights in the field,
our popcorn-salt kiss, and, half
a county south, rainless, remote,
my father's undreamt dreams
of wet, blessed dirt.

# *Waitress at a Window*

You can feel dusk suck at the heat and clatter
and rhythms of earnest conversations,
standing a minute with the silver pitcher,
letting its sweat collect in your palm
as a secret, something for yourself,
like the thought of diving on a long breath
into the swelling river, then rising to recover
and lie motionless, face upward on the water.

# *Thieves*

In any big city my father made
a point of knowing how to find skid row
and drive us slowly through.
My mother would rattle the map and complain
and reach to lock car doors, while my brother
pressed against his window, and I slid down
further in my seat, embarrassed by the solemn
exaggeration in my father's voice. Burnt-out
neon signs. Bums the color of pavement.
*Poor sons-of-bitches,* he'd always say.
*Luck will rob you a thousand ways.*
It was thirty years before I'd see
the picture of him, age five, in government-
issue overalls, posed with his brothers
by the crank Ford, under a dust-eclipsed sun.
Cropless seasons were all those kids had seen,
till that spring a thunderhead opened over them,
coaxing forty acres of decent corn.
They measured the stalks that climbed the air
for weeks, till the morning an eerier sun-darkening
clouded up from the south:
grasshoppers searching out any green spot.
In a matter of hours the corn devoured—
then fenceposts, window-curtains,
paint straight off the house; hoppers plugging
the old Ford's radiator, clogging calves' mouths
and nostrils till the animals collapsed.
Nothing left, and still
they whirred down in waves, piling up
in shady corners a foot and deeper.

*After a day you could step out in the yard*
*without getting smacked and tobacco-stained*
*by the hail of them, but the place you knew*
*was gone.* Cousins and neighbors gone soon after.
Grandpa packing up to find town-work.
Where? For how long?

Once, on vacation in New Orleans, even Mom
was too hot to keep the windows rolled up
on our detour. We felt as gritty as folks
on the street anyhow, and this section of town
wasn't the colorless smear he usually took us to:
vendors juggled oranges, and tourist-carriages
clipped through, the horses sporting straw hats
that swayed through jazz curling out
of open doors, intricate as the lacy
iron railings wound with flowers above us.
And to our amazement Dad was pulling over,
beckoning to an old guy with a cardboard sign:
TOURS. FIVE DOLLARS. A whiff
of licorice as he crawled in back with us
and talked Dad toward the cemetery
where ornate graves were stacked
above ground to keep the sea
from rising up and separating families.
Here it wasn't dust, but water
that had threatened—even the dead.
Brad and I scuffed in and out of shadows,
following lizards that flashed and vanished,
as Dad read the tiers of names to himself—who
could've wandered all the way to this sunken
swamp to die, I wondered, but Dad
was saying nothing. Trouble was, the old
fellow warned, sometimes thieves broke

*22*

into these graves, looking for whatever
they could take off the bodies, so even if
a name showed up here, the soul might be adrift.

# Leukemia

My mother's given up on her dream
of a brand-new house. *What's wrong
with what we've got,* my father doesn't
say, exactly. "Go ahead" is what he says,
not *I built this one myself, it's where
we've lived what life we can recall—
what would I do in a big new place
with nothing familiar?* Nor can she say
*It would help me.* And neither will admit
*I'm too weary for this argument.*
It's a slow leukemia she's fending off—
she could have years, and we take them
as given, rather than track this passing one
for the shadow of when she may be gone.
So, gradually she's patching new house in
over old. My father wakes disoriented under
his ceiling-fan birthday gift; bangs a hip
on the ornate chest of drawers at night.
New gleaming sink in the bathroom with no
encoded blooms of rust, and above, open wings
of a triple-lighted, three-way mirror—
she says she wants for once to see the back
of her own head. —Where her own mother must
have cupped a hand sometimes, saying *darling*.

# S n o w

—for Brad

Fifteen below and wind at sixty,
no way to get the feeder to the cattle;
they'll have to tough it out or not
till the gusting dies down—
if they weren't the neighbor's herd left
in your care you'd forget them—
no, they'd be gone, sold for the pleading
or the settlement, like everything;
you think of cutting the motor off to sit
in the tractor cab awhile, radio songs slowly
fading out as they suck the battery dry,
white nonsense scattering at the windshield
like bits of wreckage hypnotizing
till some kind of sleep comes on—
no sleeping in the house, the bedroom closed,
the kids' rooms too, you only go
to the couch and listen to television voices
calling as if to a lifeboat they don't
know anything about; once in a while the
answering machine—not her, just
your mother or sister, worried, trying to
coax you to the phone, draw you out,
but you're too tired to tell them there's
nothing left here to worry about:
if the gusting doesn't die down soon
the cold will finish all of it.

# To the Wizard

Bleached houses thinning out,
plains-gusts filling in, taking
our after-school talk and Tim
Houck's teased-mean shepherd's
barking—another day at our backs—
Janny and me blank, drifting
the empty lot before our own wan
houses toward the limits of town—
spotty switch grass, dust, yucca,
sagebrush, nothing, now
and then a piece of rose-quartz,
once a stone with shells in it.
But today—*look*—a bill
of monopoly money—*what?*
Another—a fifty—a twenty, *look*—
*the whole darn stack* flung
and blown and caught beyond
the path, prickles snagging, us
plucking white, gold, blue, pink,
green, stirring up sage scent,
scheming a spy game to match
this miraculous find, till Janny keels
over, MATH, GEOGRAPHY chucked
to the winds—*it's poppies*
*on the way to Oz*—and we're both
collapsed, waiting for the Emerald
vista, or Glynda, or the Wizard
himself—whispering to him
*this is home, look at it*—
*send us the twister, one like*

26

*we watched tip down in May—*
*don't let it veer off into the prairie*
*this time; let it do its work.*
*We can pay.*
*Take us. Don't bring us back.*

# Twisting Vines

My mother bought a dress once and my dad
said it looked like curtains. Nothing if not honest,
nothing much but me to his name, doing his best
about the trike and baby pool, new triple-speed
living-room fan, her just-landed job as a typist
while her mother baby-sat. There must
have been some wedding, or National Guard
occasion—James-Dean handsome he was,
even in eagle-crest hat, glare-polished shoes—
but the dress went right back in its creased
paper bag, unused. She had modeled it for me first
though, gazing over each shoulder to the longest
mirror before he got home, smeared and hot
from painting houses. *How does it look, hon?*—
that dress I remember more than any other,
off a rack at London's, our two-block downtown's
only clothes store. *Scoop-necked,* she called it,
*for summer. Cap-sleeved.* White, with a pattern of
little twisting green vines. I touched the satin piping
that showed off her collarbone, tiny waistline.
Made her look like a full grown fairy out of my book.
Those days she still sang when she sifted flour, folded
laundry plucked off the line by the morning
glories and tulips—"Tammy's in Love," "Blue Moon,"
"My Buddy." Never again got herself
what she wished for, if she knew.

# Half Time, Oglala High, 1970

Waiting in green-and-white pleats
in the ladies' room,
we were starting to think
this game didn't need us. Our team
would clobber them, then get ushered
from locker room to bus;
*we'd* turn back with Pam's mom
and the beaten Reservation crowd:
front entrance, dim parking lot,
dimmer broken-lighted streets.
No telling now what this chopped,
low talk in the dim bathroom was—

bead-shirted girls with
great cheekbones slouched
or sat on the sinks, looking
us over and smoking, some
swinging the high moccasins
we'd been told they liked
to hide their switchblades in.
Pam and Judy and I fixed eyes
on the stall-doors in front of us
that more smoke curled above.
Toni picked at her fingernails,
fuming for us to hurry,

but Sherry, whose platinum braid
glimmered like a crazy
challenge in there, squeezed over
to the cracked mirror by the door.

She dug the pink brush
out of her shoulder-bag,
and I groaned, but Pam shrugged:
*let her keep the stares over there—*
even the two Oglala white girls,
aloof in a corner till now, glared
as she pulled the ribbon out
and shook loose the luminous hair

that had got us free rides
from the carnies last summer.
Sherry kept right on primping
when the gaunt girl in cowboy boots
snorted, pointing her cigarette
in *my* direction: my sneakers—
the little yarn pom-poms I'd laced in—
made her hiss what sounded like
*ought to take their white legs off.*
Nowhere else to pee.
I read obscenities scraped
into the dented metal in front of me,

listening for the buzzer and the boys
back dribbling, knowing these girls
weren't there for the game, but to take
our measure—our blue-shadowed eyes
and pearl earrings, our perky routines.
How could it have come as a surprise
when Sherry leaned, lifted
another handful of hair to brush,
and a fringed arm flashed, jagged
it off, then was gone before the scream?

# Frieda's Plan

—*Yankton State Hospital, 1973*

Snow's vanishing above the condemned
tunnels, where patients sometimes
sneak down to do it. Or smoke
their smuggled weed. A little
basement heat still leaks through.
These ones sleepwalking without coats
from building to building don't
even know the tunnels are under them.
*Maybe spring will stop their coughing,*
*and I might have a chance*
*to sleep,* she writes in her
assigned journal, conjuring
plausible thoughts, since
hearing voices is what got her here.
—She pulled out too soon on Ralph,
whose quick grip would've shut her up.
Well, plenty on the Rez listen
to voices, but not so many rip through
a state cop's cheek with his own pen.
—No time done for the shit *he* was trying.
She could damn well walk down
the Interstate in December if
she wanted, forget who told her to,
or where she was headed before this
detour. —Like a dream of getting
loaded up all over again and locked
in the cinder-block Indian School,
where they cut off and burned
the little medicine pouch
her mother made to protect her.

That's fine. She's always had her own
medicine. Doesn't write that down.
Stopped talking after the trooper,
but what she knows, she knows. Like
why the lame kid who tends the birdfeeder
did what he did to his dad's skull
with a claw hammer. Who those birds
are really. And that the new so-called
teacher here drives home in her faded
jeans and crooked jaw to get
beat up on after supper. She knows too,
can see clearly, as if she's watching it,
that one of these longer evenings coming
the teacher in her sweetest tone
will arrange to take poor Tom Smith home
in her red car for supper. Her project:
Tom hunched at the next desk there,
who's been on the locked ward for fourteen
years, and who's rewinding yet again
the crackling story of "Stone Soup"
he can't get enough of—digs it out
every single day to play. *All the people*
*in the village hid away their food*
*as soon as the beggar appeared.*
What can Tom Smith have done
too long ago for anyone including him
to remember? *But when they heard*
*he could make soup from a stone,*
*they opened their doors again. One by one*
*they brought out what he knew*
*was waiting for him.* Every time
the beggar pulls off his trick,
Tom rasps that laugh she's let scrape
inside of her. Fine. She knows

she went deeper into him; now he won't
go anyplace she doesn't go. Below the dripping
windows buried passageways to nowhere show
only for this morning: a ring of broken
links crossed by cottonwood shadows.
By afternoon the patterns in the trampled snow
will fade to nothing, but an evening
is coming when Tom Smith will fold
himself into the front of the red Subaru, and
Frieda will slide in back. No need for words—
just a growl of gravel to scatter the birds.

# Medevac: East From Eagle Butte

Quivering with the rotors'
low grind inside our heads,
we lift above rusted-out cars
pulled together for living in,
above the hardware store and bingo
hall, pried-apart monkey bars
at the Agency school, and past town,
over the intersections marked off
by blue tribal trash bins.
The river tears its ragged gash
through sold-off field-squares
and irrigation circles: a ruined
game of checkers. And then, just
before the bridge, vast uncultivated
pastures of the Cheyenne River
Sioux Tribe, and the black dots
of buffalo, crawling across the grass
as though things had been
going on all along like this.

# Wounded Knee Creek: Hakiktawin's Story

Believe me, I was watching.
From under my shawl I was watching.
The medicine man did not throw dust
into an officer's face. There was no dust
on that prairie frozen hard as the creek,
where the old people said Crazy Horse
lay buried in a secret place.
As our fathers' rifles were stacked
in the circle the wagon-guns surrounded,
Yellow Bird danced the last ghost dance
steps, telling us the bluecoats' bullets
would not come toward us. Black Coyote,
the deaf one, still clutched a gun inside
his blanket, and began yelling out
what it had cost him, till a soldier
grabbed it, spun him around, and we heard
one rifle crack—then the thunder
without end: all of us running through
powder-smoke and stunted pine and blur
of terror, down toward the ravine I thought
we might still lift across like
a flock of birds rising toward the ghosts
who waited. But instead everyone was falling.
I saw my grandfather sprawl, then my brother
and grandmother too in the crooked gulch,
and then my own hip tore clear through,
and my right wrist burst as I dropped.

Afterward, the cold was good. I lay a long
time listening, till finally only the wind
could be heard, scouring coarse snow
into blizzard. After the soldier picked me up,
a small girl rolled to me, crawled into
my shawl. She curled against me, and
I closed my eyes, listening to the little
sounds she made: not words, not weeping, but
the same faint, chirping phrase—
rising and falling, as if answering itself
from a long distance.

# Seventies, USD

Cut loose from our dust-stung towns and farms,
we were daze-walking dreams of becoming
somebody else by finding out what the world
might actually be—*Slaughterhouse Five, Soul
on Ice, Zen and the Art of Motorcycle Maintenance,*
professor-speak and smoke, incense, Crosby, Stills
and Nash humming us back from class or cafeteria
along the tennis courts where maple trees torched a color
we hadn't known the faded few hundred wheatfields west
we caught rides home to on weekends with anyone
driving, preferably the long way around, not
the straight shot across the Reservation's junker-road—
bag-of-bone car-chasing dogs and tumbleweed, blank
windows, or broken, once two sunken-shouldered kids
dragging a rifle across the top of the knocked-over
trailer house never righted those four years, sometimes
one of the old ones skuffing along the gravel toward us
not seeing us—creviced face impassive as the prairie
on either side—or Tribal Police bearing down
from behind suddenly—no telling what they might
decide to pull you over for, who they thought you
could possibly be in your late-model car.

But it was a rattletrap one time—Bruce Chasing Hawk
needed riders to chip in for gas, and Pam and Neal and I
threw our bags in, not about to suggest he skirt the Rez,
though maybe he secretly hoped one of us might ask
so he wouldn't have to cross that stretch
with a carful of whites who'd never even changed a flat,
himself the only Indian—only Indian in our dorm,

hometown boy, our high school's basketball star
nobody, not even the coach, had much spoken to.
I remembered Bruce, and he might have remembered me,
from earlier, the night in grade school when his
little brother fell—got kicked, my dad said later—through
a missing riser in their basement-apartment stairs:
I was riding with Dad when the rescue squad radioed;
by the time we got there Bruce had pried loose the step,
jumped down with a towel and ropes to lift the boy;
their mother hovered at the doorway as if she weren't
quite there in the chairless living room close
with smoke and her white boyfriend's
sudden absence, banter of the Jackie Gleason show
still on with no picture. I looked away when
the men brought the limp boy up, but we heard
he came-to in the admitting room later,
then the three of them were gone—a different
direction from the boyfriend, Dad said. At sixteen
Bruce appeared in town again, alone, having learned
at Cheyenne how to shoot even bent-up hoops,
and where a kid needed to play to get a scholarship.

My folks told me to pay Bruce the gas-money
back to school, but take the bus. Now and then on
campus I'd wave; he'd raise a hand. Sophomore
year my RA and her priest took me to a Rosebud
powwow, and Bruce walked over from the bleachers
—stood next to me, one of the six whites there—
gave me a piece of fry-bread. Too much tumult
for talk anyway, we watched battered cowboy boots
dance drumbeats in the lightless gym, old women's
shawls shaking songs beyond their fringe,
till a young man with braids and a bent cheek
loomed beside us, shoved a jacket at Bruce, and

angled back through the crowd. Bruce followed him
to the door in the hall behind us, but each glanced
around again; Bruce looked at me. In both faces there
I saw the same heavy eyes and narrow chin,
and realized they were brothers. Then the door swung
open, the two of them pushed through—I felt
a rush of nausea as the red glare of late prairie sun
glinted along a rifle barrel behind them—the door
slammed shut against the drum, the dancing, the chant's
pound like the beat of my terror at turning
around—no idea if anyone had seen—or if everyone had
—much less idea how many of the chanters would
vanish that decade, uninvestigated, found face down
in gullies or pastures, one woman's hands cut off.

Father Mark's truck bumped back the Rosebud road
through gritty half light, over the river, then in
darkness across Yankton; I closed my eyes, still hearing
the big drum laid on its side, throbbing below taut
voices that rose to catch at a higher pitch before
cutting back down—saw boots circle and lift again,
worn soles flickering in and out of sight, and then—from
two years back—the startling suddenness of Bruce's
moves on the basketball court: feet and hands at a pulse
no eye could anticipate or follow—they'd think they
had him covered, and he'd show up someplace else.

# The Cliff Swallows

—*Missouri Breaks*

Is it some turn of wind
that funnels them all down at once, or
is it their own voices netting
to bring them in—the roll and churr
of hundreds searing through river light
and cliff dust, each to its precise
mud nest on the face—
none of our own isolate
groping, wishing need could be sent
so unerringly to solace. But
this silk-skein flashing is like heaven
brought down: not to meet ground
or water—to enter
the riven earth and disappear.

# II
## *Secrets*

# Fly-Fishing on Tommy's Lake

*—to Dan*

For long intervals the five of us
are silent in the little boat,
drifting, taking turns with the rod,
trying to get the trick,

let the line flick out to its end
above the water, to touch
the fly down first, as if
it's just stopped buzzing there.

I pass the rod to Nan as Tommy lifts
an oar to nudge us clear of a shallow spot—
he must think of Rachel's staying back
at the lake-house after all—*to knit booties,*

she joked. How cautious with her body, so
this second child won't be lost to them.
Nan joggles the line from a snag and we rock a bit;
some minnows shimmer out from under the boat;

a loon's evening-coming-on laugh echoes,
and we all look up. "—To *themselves* they're not spooky,"
murmurs Paul. He checks the fly before Nan casts again.
The two of them, wedged in the prow,

sit closer than they ever do.
How affair-strained years haven't
torn them utterly, no one can know.
Is it possible to get accustomed

to the lens of grief, stop noticing
the way it darkens everything?
I glance at you, then your reflection:
the long brow so like your father's glints

below the blunt end of the boat,
below your effort at looking out
to the world as it is, untouched by sorrow.
Are you watching the pines' jagged shadows?

—A wreath. A shawl drawing round us
in the dimming light. But again last night
you woke with your own crying-out,
drenched, banished from that kitchen

where your father wavered in the doorframe
with his gun—alive, giving you
this chance to stop him.
Over and over the violence of waking

to remember that it's done.
Three months he's gone. You're just trying
to have a weekend with old friends.
Out in the trees' crosshatching

cicadas begin. Nearly dark.
Nobody wants to row back in.
Nan hums a song we all years ago
knew the words to, and Tommy

takes the rod again:
hardly a change in the lake's surface
as the line *whings* and *whings* across.
That's the idea—that's what you want—

not a fish caught, but calm water.
And this single motion over and over,
approximating a delicate ease
we want to believe is nature's.

# Whitehaven

—*Barbados*

Twenty empty rooms turquoise
yellow and pink they try them
out in the mornings drink rum
at night so dark except for moon
in this honeymoon dream monkey
at the window monkey's
shadow on the bars and no one
else this end of the island but
the cook gone back home by now
salt breeze lacing in then out
of the house again a door
below bangs without latching
gauze curtain flutters open above
thin as the lone man's shirt
unbuttoned flapping at the bare
top of a hill where they braked
lean-muscled young man asked
where it was they wanted to go
told them correctly as they
would find out in ten minutes
then said give me five dollars
glanced at her purse on the seat
leaning into the moak he said it
again then more tersely
*I'm beggin' man*
in her sleep she keeps waiting
for the door to bang again

# Night Before the Fertililty Clinic

*—to Jane Ellen Harrison*

Five minutes and the lights
will black out here. The landlord
tacked notices today on every floor
that workmen will be fixing the wiring
tonight from twelve to four,
so I've brought the flashlight into bed
to keep on reading your book the way I did
detective mysteries when I was a kid,
hungry for answers amid the shadows'
whines and rattles. *The gods,* you say,
*are images of desire.* —And before the gods,
long before Homer, prayers and paeans went
to the snake goddess, poppy goddess,
Great Mother who presided at Delphi once.
Pausanias said to approach her at evening,
light the lamps, burn incense
on the hearth, lay a coin on the altar,
and into the deity figure's ear
a question could be whispered.
Then afterward, with ears covered,
hurry back along the road a little: if I took
my hands from my head what first stirring
in the dark would be the oracle?

# Stiff Heart

Another chill, fog-blank sky,
morning after the funeral,
Monday after the second suicide.
Chrysanthemum-dust coats the table
and the elbow of the suit jacket
you couldn't hang up last night.
Downstairs in the trash: the pants
and shoes stained white Wednesday
from your breaking into your mother's
running car with a can of paint.
The smells of that garage won't
let you rest—exhaust and paint
and what came over you when
finally you got to her on the seat.

After your father, months of talk.
This time, silence, exaggerating
all the Monday cacophony outside:
clanking lunchboxes and instruments,
dog howling a siren's echo,
drivers honking, gunning engines
to court date or shrink appointment.
I reach to pull the window down for
you on all of it, but up the street
comes the shattering music
of the recycling truck—
*glass, aluminum, plastic*
*glass, aluminum, plastic*—
making its way around our cul-de-sac,
as gloved men order for another use

what can be salvaged from last week,
and leave the empty green bins
waiting for us in a line.

# Secretissime, Praesentissime

*—for Mia*

Most hidden, most present, like Saint
Augustine's notion of the divine,
soul of my soul, flickering right in front
of my turning to the counter peeling
vegetables while behind shimmers this
hummingbird-jewel, most known ungraspable wing
singing "Jingle Bells" to your popsicle-
stick dolls as you serve up their pudding
of pinecone and carrot snips, miraculous
balancer on the arms of two chairs,
miraculous to have formed inside and grown past
my worry, wash hands don't take dares,
do leave, tiny propeller of sugar and ruby
and air, leave the weight of me behind, but stay.

# Secrets

—to Mia

*Even before a word is on my tongue,*
*lo, Lord, thou knowest it altogether.*
                              —Psalm 139

1.


The swans snap up the chunks of bread, then veer
away again, and you call the swans' forgotten
thank-yous across their wake. Slowly stirred
water clears, the way darkness does in your room
when I wait for my eyes to adjust,
for you to take shape under my hand.
The nightmare dissolves; I
will never know what it was.

2.

"I'm making a *secret*!" you announce,
warming and molding a piece of beeswax
with awkward little fingers, having just learned
that thrilling word I pray will never do you harm.
"Don't look," you say, "don't see it."
Then in a minute, proudly, you display
the gold-red flamelike shape.

3.

I'd forgotten the boy in London yelling
at the black swan, the only black swan I've ever seen.
He wanted it to stop nipping, bullying the other swans
away from his crumbs. *Make it go away,*
he pleaded with his father, but finally
it was the boy who went away. I stayed, watching
the black swan left alone, thinking of the black
Rosetta Stone I had been to see one last time that morning,
and shivered in December mist, wanting to be taken
away too from that place, that half light, taken back
to your father who wasn't your father yet,
whose steady voice over the phone
cleared the shadows I couldn't talk about.

4.

In "Sweet Porridge" it's a lovely secret
the girl's given: magic words to make the pot
cook up food she and her mother might die without.
And when the mother tries the spell by herself,
her *not* knowing the right order is also delightful—
porridge out the window, porridge down the walk
and through the streets of the town, so that anyone
who came in from the fields had to eat his way home.

5.

I changed the lock on my apartment,
and a whole new doorknob had to be put on.
The handyman laid all the brass pieces out
on a sheet of newspaper—delicate shapes that
would fit together precisely to let only me
into that place. While he worked, he told me
about his wife and daughter, how he didn't know
what to do to keep them apart from each other.
The door stood open, and behind him
the evergreen outside was thrashing. I pictured
the girl's freckles and spaghetti straps, thick
red hair rippling in the truck window outside
on the day Jay had come to make his estimate.
Her mom's visitation rights had been taken away
for using her as a decoy in petty robberies.
Jay and I tried to figure out what to do
with a teenage girl who refuses to talk to you.
When the lock was together, he handed me the key.

6.

Ten years I hid, at the back of my closet shelf,
a little book I'd received in a moment of fear.
I had gone with a friend in the grade ahead of me
along to her church, having no idea what the word
*evangelist* meant. The howling minister pointed me out
as one who needed saving, and my friend nudged me up
toward the altar to be touched with the water and
take the book. When I found it again I was eighteen:
just a little volume of the Psalms, but it still
unnerved me—*Thou knowest me right well;*
*my frame was not hidden from thee,*
*when I was being made in secret,*
*intricately wrought in the depths of the earth.*
*Thy eyes beheld my unformed substance;*
*in thy book were written, every one of them,*
*the days that were formed for me,*
*when yet there was none of them.*

7.

Not long before she made herself die,
before she lost herself to grief entirely,
your grandmother watched with your dad and me
the ghostly sonogram knot of you glowing
in my belly. "What a beautiful secret," she gasped,
released for a moment into astonishment.
She left no note in the mountain-house, but we kept
the cut-out shadow-birds she had hung in the windows
to keep live birds from slamming themselves into
their own reflections. She had dreamed, one night
after her husband's death, of his motioning to her
from the other side of a glass door.

8.

Some night that's coming
I'll hear your voice in my sleep
and stumble to your room to know what it is
you're calling out, but you'll be in a room
someplace else, in a body longer than mine
probably, though maybe you'll still
sleep under the quilt you love now—
patched-together scraps of my childhood curtains
and outgrown pedal-pushers, Mom's aprons, doll
dresses you fit your own dolls into
long after mine disappeared. And if someone else
is there in the room  with you, I ask only
that he love you, and the words on your tongue,
and the words still unspoken.

# The Girl Without Hands

*—Grimm*

Sure enough, I hear the old
*I told you so:*
*Now that you have a child—*

*now how do you like these stories*
*of the parents who unwittingly*
*bring their children to misery,*

*and need to be forgotten?*
What saved the girl, if saved
she was, was her weeping. And not

just once; twice the tears falling
onto her hands, then the stumps
of her hands, washed them too clean

for the devil to go near,
so he threatened her piousness
through others. The miller,

the girl's father, had no thought
of harming anyone, least of all
his daughter. What

can he have wished for but to feed
his family? When there is no grain,
a miller has nothing. Who in need

doesn't hope for a lucky turn? Who
hasn't once overlooked the glint
in a generous eye, or failed to

wonder *what could this fellow want,*
*what's standing behind my mill besides*
*the old apple tree?* He bargained it.

His daughter was what stood there
in the mill yard, sweeping.
Now when a weeping child speaks with more

authority than the parent, who has
made a grave mistake,
how can the man ashamed refuse?

*Do as the devil says: lift your axe, Father—*
*God will protect me.* Afterward he begged her
not to walk off through the heather,

but in the end it is the parents who give in.
So how was it when the king
found her pulling down

the pear with her mouth—how was it
she said to him, she who had set out
away from home so resolute,

"All save God have deserted me"?
In time she too had a child she
bundled away, the boy

named Sorrowful, refugee
hidden in the house with the sign above
"Here everyone is free."

# Mirage

*Ghosts don't exist in some cultures—*
*they think time exists.*
　　　　　　　　　—Martin Broken Leg

With a shuffle of palm leaves
Sunday School let out,
and Grandma and I took off
in the sticky-seated Oldsmobile,
heading for her home place up
beyond the Cheyenne,
swigging cream sodas and staring down
the undulating asphalt-swath
that simmered across the plain.
Flocks of grouse flared
as we roared past, and I wondered
if birds were ever tricked like us
by those dips of heat-shimmer
scattered ahead in the highway
that looked like pools of water
till the car came close.
I wasn't really taken in by them,
but felt drawn to a filmy
presence in the road—kept watching
for another one to quaver into view
as the prairie shushed
on either side of us. Grandma told me
she'd gotten seasick as a girl
rocking across the waves of grass,
driving alone in the wagon behind
her dad's, holding her mule
to the overgrown Indian trails.
When they made the journey again

in springtime, though, with her mother
and the younger kids to homestead,
the sound of the grasses that last
moonlit night carried her to the claim
like a smooth tide coming in.

I only knew Grandma as Grandma alone,
but of course she'd had a family,
and then a second one: my mother, uncle,
and aunt, and before them a husband, Earl
—her love, I imagined, whose heart
stopped before mine began. I glanced
at Grandma's thick-veined hand
on the steering wheel—the one fine
thing she owned, the opal ring
from him. It always glimmered when
her fingers moved, as though it might
disappear if you stopped looking.
The stone had come from my grandfather's
father, she said—from a tie-tack
the old man had won in a poker game,
and brought as a gift to the wedding
of the son who wouldn't speak to him.
For an instant I saw, through the stacked
depths of years, faces of fathers,
and fathers' fathers—and mothers too,
sober and dark as in old photographs,
puzzled and puzzling and making
me feel lightheaded, staring down
through all those lives.
Then it closed, and the faces
were nothing again—*Where
do you think Grandpa is
now, Grandma?* I asked, in my head,

as another swell wavered into layers
and vanished. But *heaven* would have been
her answer, and I'd had enough of heaven
that morning. I leaned my face out
to the grasses, to the rippling air—
let it knock my white straw hat
into the back seat.

# Black Walnut

I gripped my mother's small, rough hand,
as with her other hand she tried to hold
herself steady on the table
while the doctor cranked a drill into her hip
to draw out marrow. *Let it be clean,*
I said silently over and over, trying
not to faint. No way to imagine grasping
my friend Sheila's hand three months later
in the same scene. Yesterday Sheila
shaved off her few remaining tufts of hair—
they kept creeping out from under her wig,
not quite the same color. We talked it over
on the phone while I watched my sprawled daughter
draw a face and hands jumping rope
with a rainbow, needing no hair, no body either.

Class over, and my conference after
with the boy who keeps turning in suicide poems.
Vivid, convincing poems. Finally I asked
if he has a psychiatrist. He does, he said,
then stood up, knocking my cold coffee over.
Now his slicker descends the wet steps outside,
and I pull on my own trenchcoat and scarf, then
sit back down at the scarred, empty table.
This is the time of morning my mother will walk
her little dog out through hard-packed
South Dakota snow, leash tight in a mittened fist,
rapid steps quickening the blood that
threatens her. I've never sat in this room alone
before, or noticed what kind of tree shadows

the window behind my students' shoulders,
its rain-darkened leaves dripping below the sill.

# Dreams

Why rehearse for slowly splintering to bits,
forgetting the way your mother braided
your hair, which turn to take to pick
your daughter up from day care, the room,
the sleeve where your husband's hand first
touched your shoulder, even the fact that you
have hands, that hands know how to reach
for the light switch, if only they'd remember.
Who needs these dreams, when you've had practice
enough—they're just a time-lapse version
of what happened whenever your father screamed—
except now you never find the topmost
closet shelf to scramble up to, dark cubby
you squeezed yourself far back inside,
so only echoes of the shattering
could get to you. Better—as if you had
a choice—those dreams of remembering what
never really happened, your mother lacing white
ribbons in your braids while Uncle Buddy crooned
Sinatra tunes, or the cattle nudging up
against the fence at Bud's burial, as though
to calm you. But usually what you
thought you knew starts peeling off
in the dark, truth evaporating
as wind shears in through the open car-window
and the moon blurs under the surface of a cloud.
Levin's pages tear loose, flutter away
from *Anna Karenina*. The spinning tilt-a-whirl's
fuses blow, your dear friend's gone for good one
night in his crushed sky-blue Camaro.

Silk scarves of every color pull free
from the stand on the Ponte Vecchio
to dazzle the Arno with reflections spun out
like a ripped-apart rainbow, and the sweat-
and-barn scent of your father's workshirt's
simply gone, distilled to nothing, as you
try to somehow fit your head there, to find
a way that's safe to rest.

# Freud's Study: Anna Packing Up

*We are no longer quite here and not yet there at all.*
　　　　　　—Anna Freud, on the family's awaited exile
　　　　　　from Vienna to London, May 25, 1938

*The triumphant feeling of liberation is mingled too strongly
with mourning, for one had still very much loved the prison
from which one has been released.*
　　　　　　—Sigmund Freud's first letter from London,
　　　　　　to Max Eitingon, June 6, 1938


Far from the city's clock calibrated to awaken
hammering mannequins; far from the echo-tricking
tunnel passages lacing beneath strictly
divided-off streets—smell of hot chestnuts, jokes,
snickers, people gossiping with their fingertips in the mist
near bier halls and galleries, or within, before nightmare
Dürer and Cranach,  Klimt's evanescent spills,
the thousand-faceted mirror-gowns of undoing;
far from his cherished chanson-allurements,
"La Soularde" rasping out a half-open door
like smoke filtering through crooks and turns
of the Innere Stadt toward the zoological garden,
keepers leaning at the entrance near-asleep, as someone
runs past late to a funeral in the Leopoldstadt—
the temple across from the tailor twice ransacked
in a week—chilblained sweepers' hands held out behind
the news kiosk; far even from the *Jude*-scrawled
Alsergrund walls, the Berggasse right out front, Martin
in the vestibule boxing up Papa's files, Mother washing
linens the Gestapo yanked down from her closet,
still carrying in her apron pocket lost Sophie's toppled old
wunderblock; apples baking; Jo-Fi's one bark; silence under
the waiting-room prints, Boullonge's *Four Elements*—

beyond both sets of padded consulting-room doors—
one way in and another out, so no patient need admit
there might be others who visit—this room at the back
with its single door in only, and nobody here
to see my dismantling but these diminished ones
I used to sneak in to wonder at, lined up
before the books and across the maze-woven rug:
polished shadows in a place too dim for shadows, priceless,
mutilated faces staring, in front, behind, to the side,
impassive—the headless ones too—standing, sitting, one
nursing the child-god Horus, one a baboon,
one bird-bodied, hunkered down, gazing out
like the rest, stiff, unchanging, indifferent about whose
hands they might fall to if we're lost—even Eros
from Myrnia who feints perpetually left
and the Chinese sage tilting his head, stifling a grin
above the smoking implements that eat Papa's jaw—
all these unmoved, overlooking, expectant, still toe the line
of passionate angular script on the desk before them,
where a look up in any direction meets a look back
and is turned again to work. Even a glance sideways
to the study window at the left—horses stamping to drink
at the fountain below, glint of Aunt Minna's sash
opening at an angle across the inner courtyard—
the eye catches between the two center panes,
where double handles, never turned, serve as hooks
for the face-sized mirror there, the look back in.

# The Waving Window

I'm scuffing backward as I do each day
along the cracked churchyard sidewalk, too grand
a smile, too A-OK as I guess my way,
hoping little Jessie is still keeping her hand

off your plaid hairbow. Inside you've got
your plaid shoulders steady now above
the tiny chair, braced at the spot
where through the winter we have

blown on the window to draw a heart, a small
secret to float there through the morning. What
will we do in spring? Now all
alone you're balancing up there, but I'm caught

at the turn where I always disappear:
suddenly you're saying something over and
over that I can't make out. No doubt the entire
nursery can hear, but I, who should be tuned

to the inaudible, all I can do is stop. Then turn:
is the tattered man I nearly trampled
Friday back there with his torn
sleeping bag against the door of the chapel?

No. Like a dream I had forgotten him. And again slip
from the world I'm standing in, puzzling at your hand
still hanging behind the glass, your lips
opening and closing on a word I can't imagine.

I take one step and mouth the sounds
of LOVE, but that's not it. Not love?
I shrug, tilt, then clatter back across the stones,
take the steps two together, shove

open the weighted door, kneel down: over
you scamper to whisper *take off your glove.*

# Mother Listening

In the next room the child can't go to sleep
she keeps taking deep breaths—*I can't*
*stop doing this* she said as you sat with her
on the cloud sheets and tried to gingerly

she keeps taking deep breaths—*I can't*
answer her questions about if it hurts this much
on the cloud sheets and tried to gingerly
when you have a baby and whether it's possible

answer her questions about if it hurts this much
she might ever see again
when you have a baby and whether it's possible
her best friend who died three weeks ago

she might ever see again
you tried *Pippi Longstocking* to shift her focus
her best friend who died three weeks ago
she's still swallowing the dark in gulps though

you tried *Pippi Longstocking* to shift her focus
today at the mall you snapped at her
she's still swallowing the dark in gulps though
impatience you wanted that moment to stop

today at the mall you snapped at her
her demands then you bought her
impatience you wanted that moment to stop
a stuffed dog like the one her friend

her demands then you bought her
dragged everywhere it lies beside her now
a stuffed dog like the one her friend
off-kilter cartoon eyes staring into hers

dragged everywhere it lies beside her now
*stop doing this* she said as you sat with her
off-kilter cartoon eyes staring into hers
in the next room the child can't go to sleep

# Okobojo: Light Moving

Huge prairie sky, late-day tumbling light,
six of us in the van, and this driving
like flying, a kind of stasis
in landscape changeless to the horizon,
where it seems there's nothing else
of the world. The van picked up by
light's commotion, its metal reflecting,
entering blue-violet-pink, shot-silk
rippled out from the west, immense
tossing mane of a weightless horse
whose force rolls under: waterfall
flinging sparks toward the moon rising
opposite. Ninety-seven degrees, wind
at twenty, air dry as the dust it suspends,
the broad light rushing slows down
everything else, confuses shadows
beneath: meadowlarks dip into wind
and disappear; fenceposts there and gone,
there and gone again; blistered barns
and houses nearly sunk in waves
of clarity, then shade. Blunt, Onida
past, lost little towns stuck behind us,
their grit left between our teeth;
twelve miles west, two south: Okobojo
Creek Cemetery, another patch of plain
where nothing changes: sharp scent
of sage, switch grass–spikes, cicada-whir
hold steady as we step out to pressure
of heat. "Up a piece this road is where
old Arlen Voss used to keep his sofa

in the ditch." —Aunt Marilyn, not budging
from the back seat, pipes up with this,
as Mom squints past barbed wire. He'd sit
and watch for the weather coming, she says.
The sky his own TV that never signed off:
brilliant shifts, loomings of news his life
depended on, like these lost lives beneath
the markers, Ora Tagg, Leo Sommer, Nels
Wickstrom, others nameless as the grass,
or noted in the mailbox at the gate—the list
of lives, for some even what it was
that stopped them: diphtheria, rattler bite,
lightning, throat infection, gunshot wounds,
accidental and not—short lives, long
lives the clouds have gathered over,
blazing, darkening their stones and silences.
A meadowlark's four notes mark our own
silence—my father, my uncle, my young
daughter and me, wiping dirt from carved
letters, kicking at thistle the same shade
as that pink streak running northwest now
like a sudden gash—the murdered wife's
bonnet-sash blown back. Finally Frederick—
Mia spots it—my father's and my uncle's
grandfather, whose wife Lovisa traveled home
again to Sweden to find, bring him to this
place where now they lie either side of their
eldest, Leonard, a hooligan, another murdered
one. Or else they've gone, like the horse
that buckled over us and vanished—washed
and taken by purple torrent and blaze—
Dad says something about moving the three
graves to town, where they'd be cared for,
be with the rest of the family (and what he

76

doesn't say: where he'd be with them, Uncle
Norm too, before long). Norm shakes his head,
seems to shiver at the thought of stirring up
all that granite and dirt and bone; Dad yanks
out the rest of the weeds blocking the name.
Mom calls from the van, and he looks over to
the west—she doesn't like him driving after
dark any more. Soon the only light left
will be the still moon behind us.

# The Blue Table

*—for Philip Geiger*

In the polished hall
a young man leans beside
a blue table—head bent
as if to listen, as if just
the right angle of concentration
might brace his mother whom
he cannot watch stepping off-kilter
past shadow into windowlight.
She's making her way toward the last
room, one step, another, struggling
to match her steps to the floor
that lists like the deck
of a ship beneath her, leaving
him behind in the foreground,
and his sister on the sofa—wrecked,
a doll thrown down.
He knows his mother will not look back
as she enters the room beyond
the windows. He knows he will follow.
All he wants, though,
is to stay where he is, and run
his hand along the blue enamel
from end to end.

# The Tuesday Healing Service,
# Saint Mark's Mission Church

*Nothing lives long,*
*only the earth and the mountains*
—Lakota death song

The woman with the blue felt hat and no
hair beneath it runs a finger along
each faint eyebrow. Further down the pew
a man turning his gold ring

around, around, keeps his eyes
closed until the moment
the minister lifts his head and rises
to begin the old intonations: *Who sent*

*His only* and *We beseech; Deliver us;* then *Dry bones,*
*dry bones.* Blessed release of mind from
thought as the rhythm's crucible turns,
*and behold, a rattling; and the bones came*

*together, bone to its bone. And as I looked,*
*there were sinews upon them,* and then the skin,
the breath, the hope mended, the unlocked
graves, the people gathered whole again,

changed. The voice descends; the sexton holds
the altar gate open for the Reverend, who, bowing
his head, passes everyone, the green and red and gold
brocade sheen of his stole

like frost-altered leaves that hang
outside the massive chapel door—
leaves that in another week will be smoldering.

# Leonids

*—Buck's Elbow Mountain, Virginia,*
*November 2001*

Far from the city, above the fog, at four we woke Mia
and climbed with flashlights to the roof
where Allen already stared up from his sleeping bag;

we lay down on our backs alongside him,
Mia between us, all huddling under spruce-torn wind
in parkas and blankets and pulled-down stocking caps,

letting our eyes adjust and watch as we saw ourselves
get sifted through the long-gone comet's swath—
bit by burning bit of antique debris,

razor-slits of ice like thought-chips igniting the dark,
streaking over every second or two or three,
untimeable intervals, from every unexpected angle

across the vast black field that seemed a place
we might fall toward without fear of being lost—like my
body falling to yours in the dark, in desire, yet farther,

to be caught by this wavering light-net. Still your
shoulder's curve held the back of my head; my belly
held Mia's; through your bones I heard you answer

Allen's questions about what passed before, around
us—and what comes into vision when we don't
gaze directly, when we look away. For some time then

only wind could be heard. If one ember had ripped
toward us from the radiant-point, we wouldn't have known—
we were vanished anyway in each meteor

gleaming and fading before the next, no sense of the hours,
our shivering bodies remote, until a long flare
with a corkscrew-tail seared over, and seemed to howl—*like*

*a fireworks-squeal,* whispered Mia, still awake after all.
*What is it* said Allen, as howls echoed, pitching higher and
higher, and you told him *it's the coyotes*—Gertrude

down the road had said they'd found their way here—
who knows how. I should've known that twisting prairie-wail
from childhood—now somewhere out in the lower field
     their eyes

glimmered, answering the sky. After a while they quieted;
daylight began dimming it all; we found ourselves finding
our way back down to bed. In my strange morning-sleep

after-images glowed—like what I see sometimes when I've
closed my eyes and still have your eyes before me, light
     distilled
to a purer light, light I'll fall toward in the dark when I die.

# Notes

p. 10   "Homesteaders": The Homestead Act of 1862 promised ownership of a 160-acre tract of public land in the West to any head of a family who staked a claim, cleared and improved the land, and lived on it for five years.

p. 12   "Regardless of the Final Score": The account of Sitting Bull's assassination is recorded in *Bury My Heart at Wounded Knee*, by Dee Brown.

p. 13   "Keith's Dream": Herbert Zitcalazi was the four-year-old son of Yellow Bird, medicine man at Wounded Knee at the time of the massacre of 1890. He is quoted in *The Ghost-Dance Religion and Wounded Knee*, by James Mooney.

p. 26   "To the Wizard": The poem refers to *The Wizard of Oz*, icon of American culture, by L. Frank Baum. Like many of my generation, I grew up knowing the MGM movie which was shown on TV every year, and became acquainted only as an adult with Baum's books, and still later with his work in South Dakota during the period before and after the Wounded Knee Massacre, when, as editor of *The Aberdeen Saturday Pioneer,* he wrote fanatical editorials advocating "total annihilation of the few remaining Indians" in the Dakotas.

p. 35 "Wounded Knee Creek: Hakiktawin's Story": Hakiktawin was another of the few Lakota witnesses who survived the Wounded Knee Massacre. Her account can be found in Dee Brown's *Bury My Heart at Wounded Knee*.

p. 37 "Seventies, USD": "During those two years [1973–1975] more than sixty Indians on the Pine Ridge reservation—some say as many as three hundred—died violent and unexplained deaths, overwhelmingly from activity instigated by our own federal government...as a means of control and domination, some believe acting on behalf of energy interests planning to purloin the reservation's vast untapped mineral wealth, especially uranium."—Ramsey Clark, preface to *Prison Writings*, by Leonard Peltier. Rosebud and Pine Ridge are neighboring reservations in southwestern South Dakota. For the history of these events I am also indebted to Peter Matthiessen's *In the Spirit of Crazy Horse*. Chasing Hawk is a name that goes back to stories of visions seen by the Sioux delegation Red Cloud sent west in the winter of 1889-1890, to learn more about the Ghost-Dance Religion. Chasing Hawk, one of their people who had died not long before, was seen by the delegates, coming toward them from a very large buffalo-skin tipi, inviting them and all friends to live with him (*The Ghost-Dance Religion and Wounded Knee*, James Mooney).

p. 46 "Whitehaven": A moak is a small, open vehicle used for transportation on Barbados.

p. 47 "Night Before the Fertility Clinic": The quotation comes from *Ancient Art and Ritual*, by Jane Ellen Harrison.

p. 48 "Stiff Heart": Emily Dickinson's poem #341 is the source of the title. Her lines read, "The stiff Heart questions was it He, that bore, / And Yesterday, or Centuries before?"

p. 50   "Secretissime, Praesentissime": The title is a phrase from Book One of Saint Augustine's *Confessions*. For bringing this passage to my attention, as well as for ideas central to "Leonids," I am grateful to Dan O'Neill and his work on science and spirituality.

p. 62   "Mirage": The epigraph belongs to Reverend Martin Broken Leg, Professor of Native American Studies at Augustana College, and a member of the Rosebud Sioux Tribe. His address to an audience of Lutheran pastors "on the subject of the Native American/White culture gap" is quoted in *Dakota*, by Kathleen Norris.

# The Author

**Debra Nystrom**

was born in Pierre, South Dakota. She is the author of
one previous book, *A Quarter Turn*, and her work has
appeared in *The American Poetry Review, Ploughshares, The
Yale Review,* and *The Threepenny Review*, among other
publications. Her poetry has received numerous awards,
including a post-graduate Hoyns fellowship, the James
Boatwright Prize from *Shenandoah*, the HEArt/Borders
Books Poetry Prize, and individual artist's grants from
the Virginia Commission for the Arts. She lives in Char-
lottesville, Virginia, with her husband and daughter, and
teaches at the University of Virginia.